MY FIRST PIANO *Adventure*®

FOR THE YOUNG BEGINNER

by Nancy and Randall Faber

Hi! I'm Tap, the music firefly.
See you in the pages ahead!

This book belongs to: ___george___

ISBN 978-1-61677-620-6

Art Direction: Terpstra Design, San Francisco, CA
Illustrations: Lisa Perrett, Charleston, SC

Tap's Message to You

TAP

Hi. It's me, TAP. In this Writing Book, we'll play music games to train our EARS and our EYES.

I have two friends for you to meet.

TUCKER

This is TUCKER. He loves to LISTEN. Tucker listens for high and low sounds, and short and long sounds.

What part of your body do you use to listen?

BLINKER

This is BLINKER. She has big eyes and loves to LOOK. Her eyes always watch the page to see how music notes travel.

What part of your body do you use to look?

Let's get started. Grab your pencil and come on in!

Contents

* The CD is included with the Lesson Book.

Be the Teacher!
Posture at the Piano

1. Circle the pictures that best match the words.

2. Put an X through the pictures that do not. Tell your teacher what needs to be improved!

Which Carlos?

Sit straight and tall on the front part of the bench.

or

Which twin?

With arms straight, your knuckles should touch the fallboard. Adjust the bench, as needed.

or

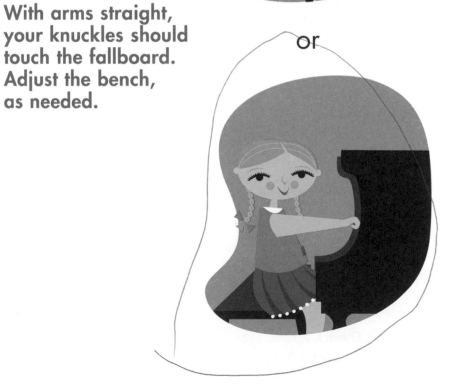

Which Dallas?

Put your hands in your lap. Is your back still straight?

or

Which Katie?

Now balance a small stuffed animal on your head. Can you count to 10 keeping your great posture?

1 2 3 4 5 6 7 8 9 10 !

Mrs. Razzle-Dazzle

Secret Message
Imitating Rhythm Patterns

Teacher: Depress the pedal and knock these rhythms underneath the keyboard.

Pretend you and a friend are exploring a dark castle. For fun, TURN OUT THE LIGHTS!

1. Your teacher will knock a secret message to you. Knock back the **same message** on the wall.

2. When you have tapped back all the messages, the trumpets will sound! Circle a trumpet each time you do this activity.

Castle Trumpets:

**It's me, Tucker.
I love to LISTEN.**

Soft or Loud? Short or Long?

Ear-training:

1. Listen to the sound your teacher plays.
   Circle one animal that fits the sound.

2. Can you make up sounds for your teacher to guess?

Soft	Loud		Short	Long

1.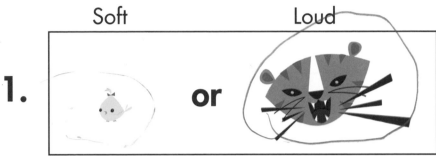

2.

3.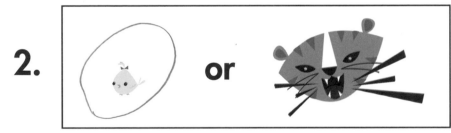

4.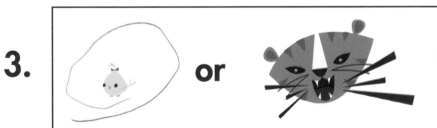

5.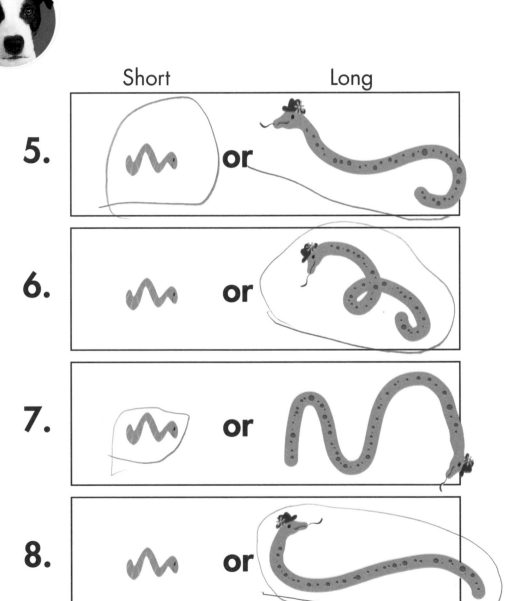

6.

7.

8.

The teacher plays his/her own keyboard examples.
Examples 1–4, soft or loud. Examples 5–8, short or long.

Your Left Hand Picture
L.H. Finger Numbers

1. Trace your LEFT HAND in the box.

2. Then connect each ring to the matching finger.
   Hint: There may be more than one ring per finger.

Your Right Hand Picture

R.H. Finger Numbers

1. Trace your RIGHT HAND in the box.

2. Then connect each ring to the matching finger.

3. Can you tap a secret message on Tap?
   Use any fingertip. Your teacher will imitate.

Make up sounds to tell this musical story.
(Your teacher may demonstrate.)

Use L.H. 3-1
"donut" position

A Bike Ride Story
Creating with Lower Sounds

A young 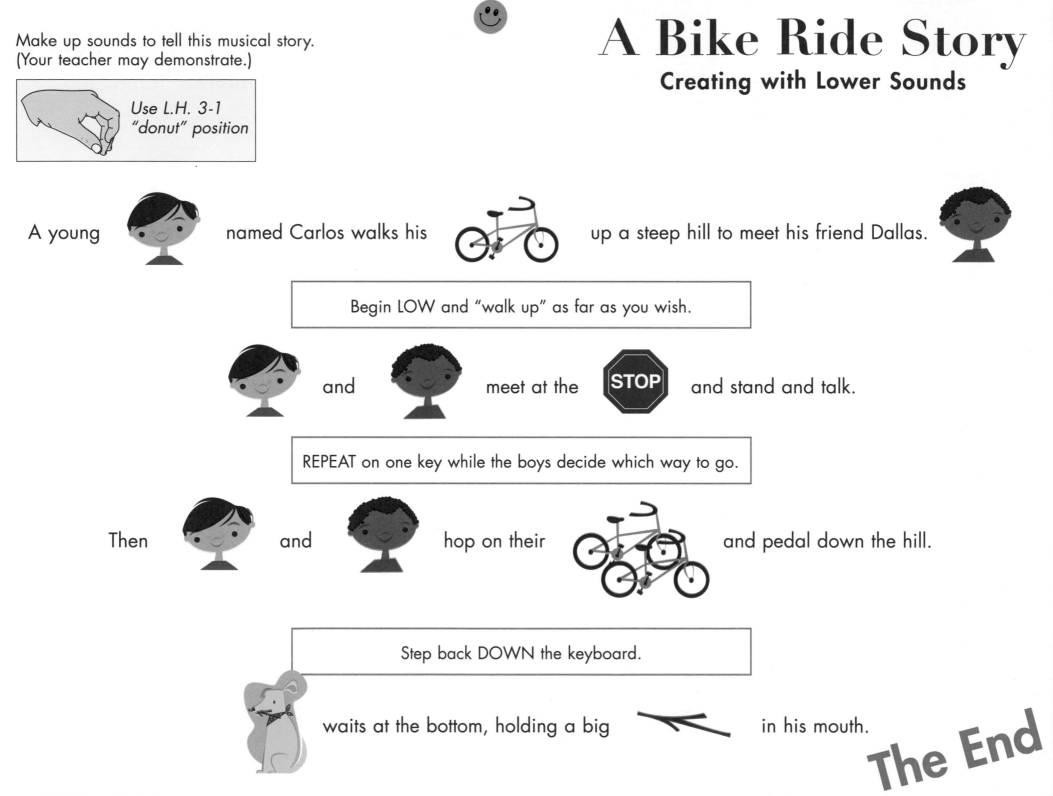 named Carlos walks his up a steep hill to meet his friend Dallas.

Begin LOW and "walk up" as far as you wish.

and meet at the **STOP** and stand and talk.

REPEAT on one key while the boys decide which way to go.

Then and hop on their and pedal down the hill.

Step back DOWN the keyboard.

waits at the bottom, holding a big in his mouth.

The End

Now make up sounds to tell this
musical story.

Use R.H. 3-1
"donut" position

A little [girl] named Katie gets her [jump rope] and hops down the [steps]

Begin HIGH and "hop down the keys."

[girl] jumps in place in the warm [sun] while she waits for the [bus]

REPEAT on one key—8 jumps in place!

When the [bus] appears, [girl] runs back up the [steps]

and grabs her [backpack] for [school] .

Step quickly back UP the keyboard to end.

The End

MORE STORIES: You may enjoy adding
to these stories or creating some of your own.

What's in the Honey Pot?

(8)

Technique: Finger Independence

On the closed keyboard lid or other flat surface:

1. With the CD or your teacher singing, do the hand motions shown below. SAY and PLAY the **L.H. finger numbers.**

2. Repeat the song using your **R.H.**

Close your hand.

What's in the honey pot
Gooey and sweet?
Little honey bees have had a treat.

Open your hand.

Busy, buzzy, buzzing
One takes a dive.

Play and say finger numbers.

1__ 2__ 3 4 5
hold   hold

Teacher Melody:

What's in the hon-ey pot goo-ey and sweet?   Lit-tle hon-ey bees have had a treat.   Bus - y buzz-y, buzz-ing,

One	takes a	dive.	1__	2__	3 4 5
Right	to	you.	5__	4__	3 3 2
Right	to	me.	5__	4__	1 2 3
To	my	door.	5__	1__	2 3 4
Hon-ey	bee	fun.	5__	4__	3 2 1

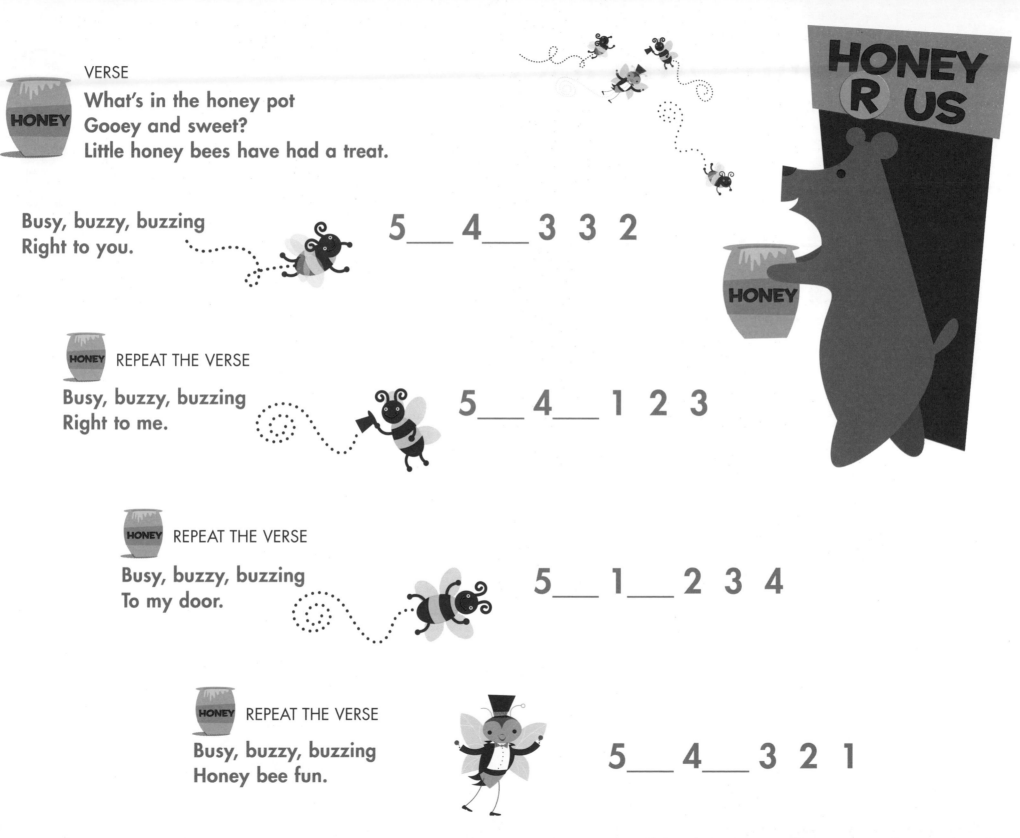

VERSE

What's in the honey pot
Gooey and sweet?
Little honey bees have had a treat.

Busy, buzzy, buzzing
Right to you.

5___ 4___ 3 3 2

REPEAT THE VERSE

Busy, buzzy, buzzing
Right to me.

5___ 4___ 1 2 3

REPEAT THE VERSE

Busy, buzzy, buzzing
To my door.

5___ 1___ 2 3 4

REPEAT THE VERSE

Busy, buzzy, buzzing
Honey bee fun.

5___ 4___ 3 2 1

HONEY R US

Pack Your Suitcase!
Two and Three Black Keys

LOW

Mrs. Razzle-Dazzle says: (pp. 14–15)

1. Color all the 2-black-key groups **RED**.
   Color all the 3-black-key groups **BLUE**.

2. Then connect each friend's suitcase to a matching black-key group.

HIGH

3. How many friends do you recognize on these two pages?

It's me, Blinker.
I love to LOOK.

Eye-training:

1. After doing *Mitsy's Cat Back* on p. 25 in your Lesson Book, look carefully and circle all the great cat-back **wrist motions**.

2. Put an X through the ones that would bother Mrs. Razzle-Dazzle!

Blinker Sees the Cat
Technique: Upward Wrist Motion

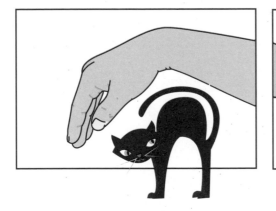

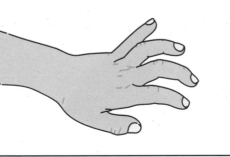

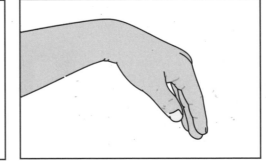

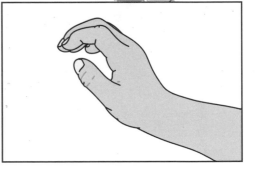

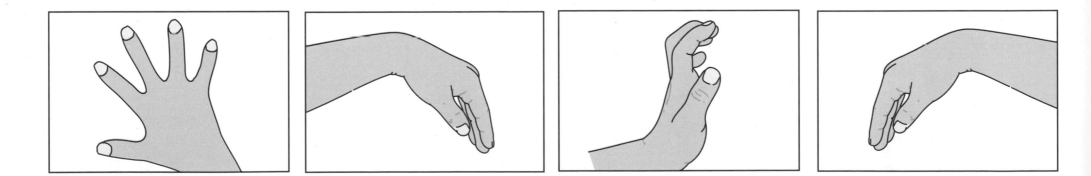

LISTEN

Ear-training:

1. Listen to the sounds your teacher plays. Is the kangaroo moving LOWER, HIGHER, or staying the SAME?

2. Circle the "roo" that matches!

Kangaroo BOINGS!
Lower, Same, or Higher

LOWER   SAME   HIGHER

Teacher plays his/her own examples going LOWER, HIGHER, or REPEATING a key.

Mother, May I?
Forte and Piano Game

Write your name BIG and BOLD on the **forte** line.

Mother, may I?

YES, you may!

$\boldsymbol{f}$ means LOUD GEORGE

Write your name small and light on the **piano** line.

Mother, may I?

YES, you may!

$\boldsymbol{p}$ means **soft** GEORGE

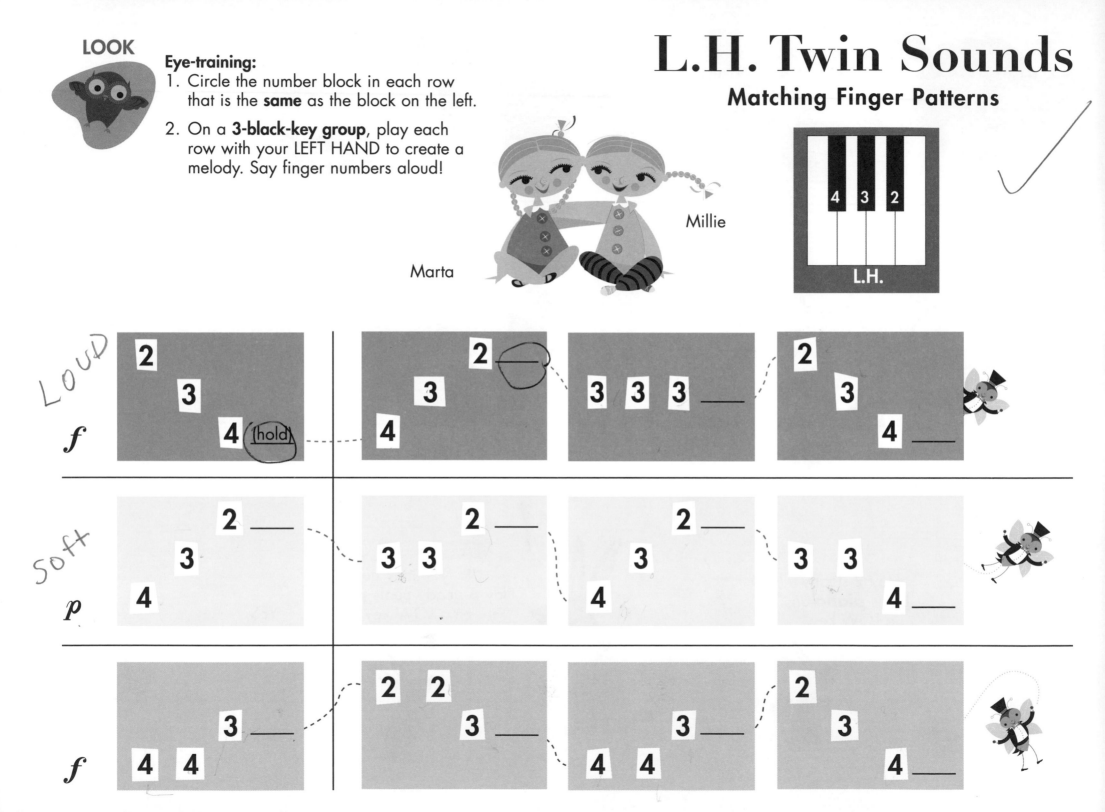

R.H. Twin Sounds

Matching Finger Patterns

1. Circle the number block in each row that is the **same** as the block on the left.

2. On a **3-black-key group**, play each row with your RIGHT HAND to create a melody. Say finger numbers aloud!

Who is who?

2 3 4

R.H.

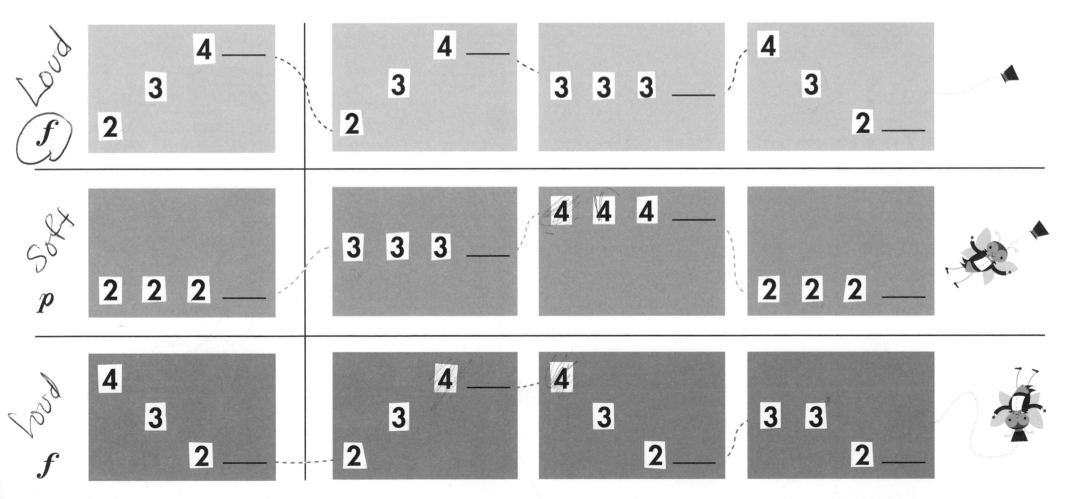

Buckle My Shoe 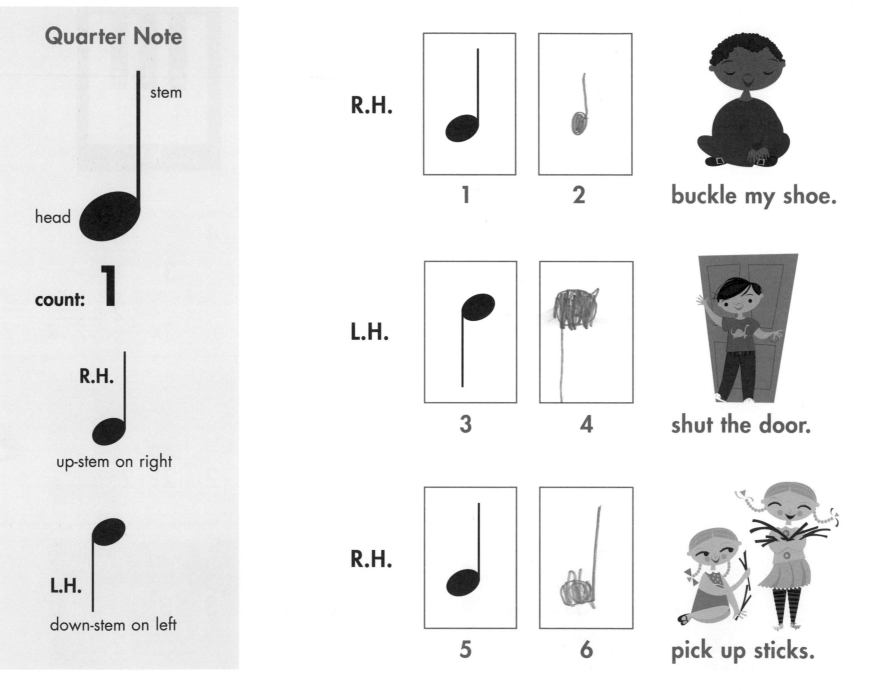 19

Feeling the Quarter Note

1. Draw a **quarter note** in each box.
2. Tap the quarter notes with the correct hand and say the rhyme with your teacher.

Quarter Note

stem

head

count: 1

R.H.

up-stem on right

L.H.

down-stem on left

R.H.

1 2 **buckle my shoe.**

L.H.

3 4 **shut the door.**

R.H.

5 6 **pick up sticks.**

L.H.

7   **8**   lay them straight

R.H.

9   **10**   a big fat hen!

DUET FUN

3. Play hands together on the **2-black-keys** for each quarter note. Use fingers 2-3.

Teacher Part: (Student plays on higher 2-black-key groups.)

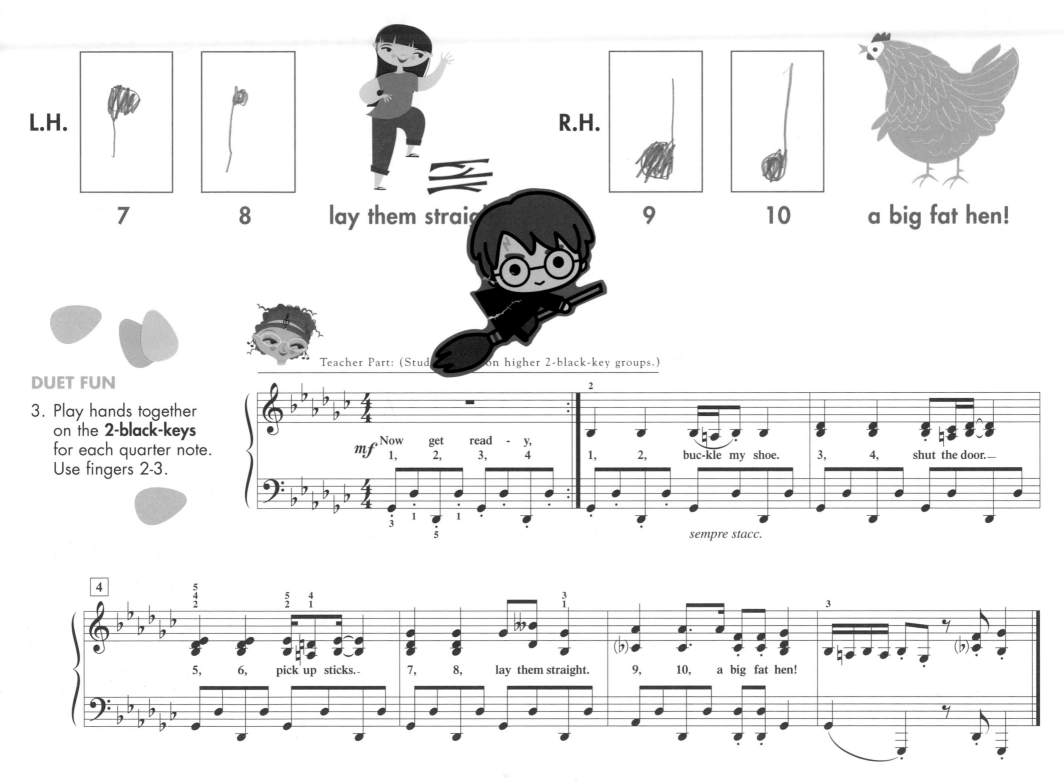

mf Now get read - y, 1, 2, 3, 4

1, 2, buc-kle my shoe. 3, 4, shut the door.

sempre stacc.

5, 6, pick up sticks. 7, 8, lay them straight. 9, 10, a big fat hen!

LOOK

Eye-training:
Even in the dark, Blinker can see if the notes move UP, DOWN, or stay the SAME.

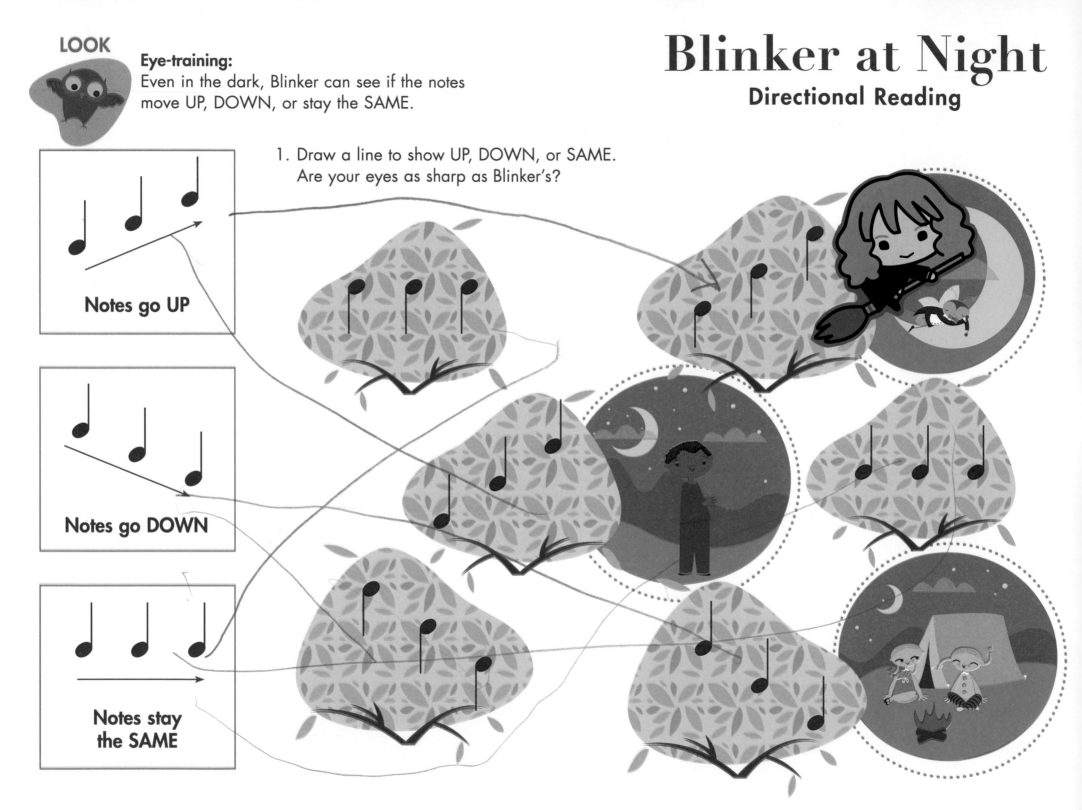

1. Draw a line to show UP, DOWN, or SAME.
   Are your eyes as sharp as Blinker's?

Notes go UP

Notes go DOWN

Notes stay the SAME

Ear-training:

Tucker hears dogs howling at night.

1. Are the howls going UP, DOWN, or staying the SAME?

2. Circle the pink poodle or dalmation for what your teacher plays.
(Teacher creates keyboard examples.) *

Tucker's Pals

Higher, Lower, Repeated Sounds

* Examples need not be stepwise. Use larger intervals to emphasize higher and lower.

Outer Space Friends

C - D - E Key Names

1. Your friends have discovered notes in outer space.
   Connect each **note** and **letter** to the correct key on the space ship.

2. Then play each note with the correct hand.
   Hint: Is the stem going up or down?

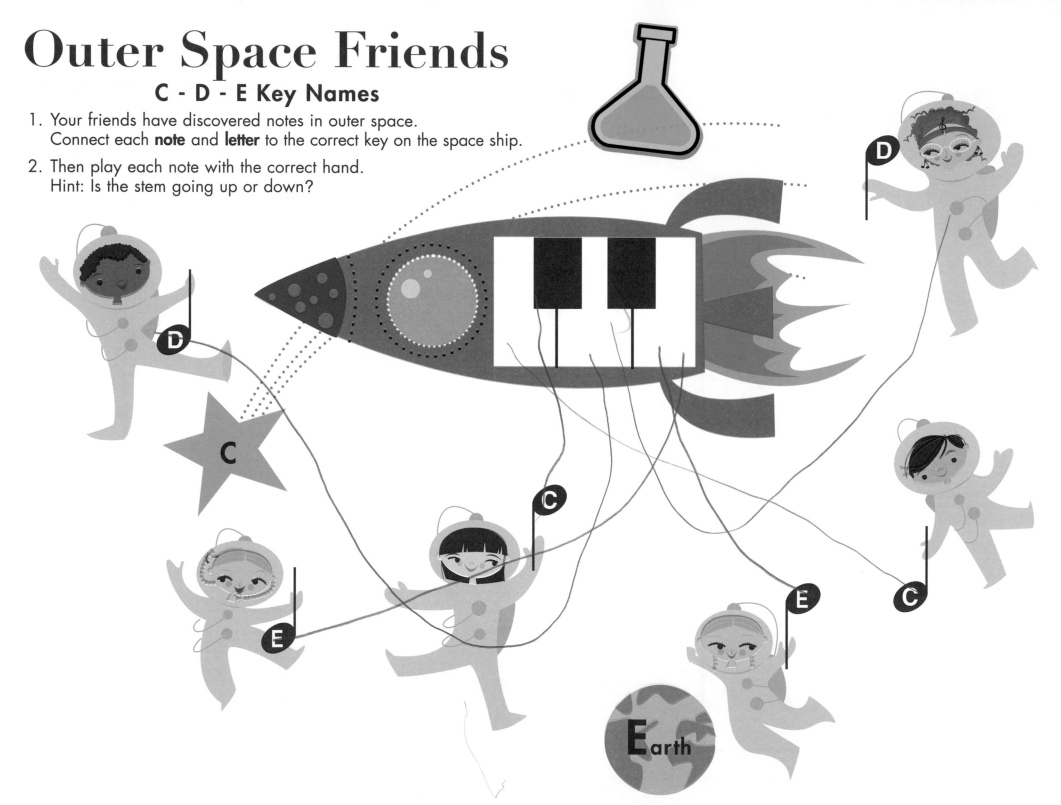

Note: The teacher may depress the damper pedal as the student plays.

Tap Composes
C - D - E across the Keys

Play the keys to tell the story.
A gold star is your signal to play.

There once was a bug who loved to play C's.
He played only C's across the keys.

PLAY

Then one day he discovered the key right BETWEEN the 2-black-keys.
(What was it?)

So then the bug switched to play only D's.
He made big leaps across the keys.

PLAY

One day he landed and slipped on the key just to the RIGHT of the 2-black-keys.
(What was it?)

PLAY

He played a soft E, **PLAY** he played a loud E, but something still was not right on the keys.

He put his little bug leg to his head, thought for a moment and then he said,

"I'll put them together, one after another and compose a C-D-E song for my mother!"
(father)

Now make up a tune on keys C-D-E.
End on a C for your fine melody!

PLAY

Rescue the Kitty

Composing Activity

1. Compose your own melody on **C-D-E**. Write finger numbers **2 3** or **4** in each box.*

2. Now play and say/sing finger numbers while the kitty sleeps.

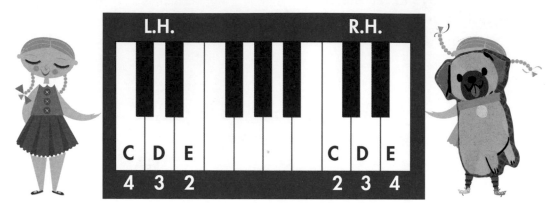

Words by Crystal Bowman

Kit - ty	cat,	where	are	you	go - ing?
Here's some	milk,	what's	your	de -	sire? _____

f

Ex: L.H.

* Your teacher may help you write.

Ex:

Trace the repeat sign.
(thin line, thick line, and two dots)

R.H.

p

| It's | so | dark, | the | wind | is | blow | - ing. |
| Kit | - ty's | sleep | - ing | by | the | fire. _____ |

1620

29

Turkey Talk

Feeling the Half Note

Half Note

stem

head

count: **1-2**

R.H.

up-stem on right

L.H.

down-stem on left

gobble!

1. Draw a **quarter note** in each **ORANGE** box.
   Then tap a steady ♩ beat as your teacher sings the song.

2. Draw a **half note** in each **BLUE** box.
   Then tap a steady ♩ beat as your teacher sings the song.

Ex:

Ex:

Teacher: Sing and play. Tap with L.H. while playing to guide the student.

The tur - key is a fun - ny bird, his head goes wob - ble wob - ble. And

1. Tap:

2. Tap:

MOVEMENT ACTIVITY (OPTIONAL)

1. Sit on the floor with legs crossed, like Dallas and Marta.

2. Practice setting a steady beat by alternately tapping on each knee.
   Then listen to the song and tap with these motions.
   Straighten and shake both legs at the end and say, "Run, turkey run."

3. Repeat, tapping a steady ♩ beat on your lap.

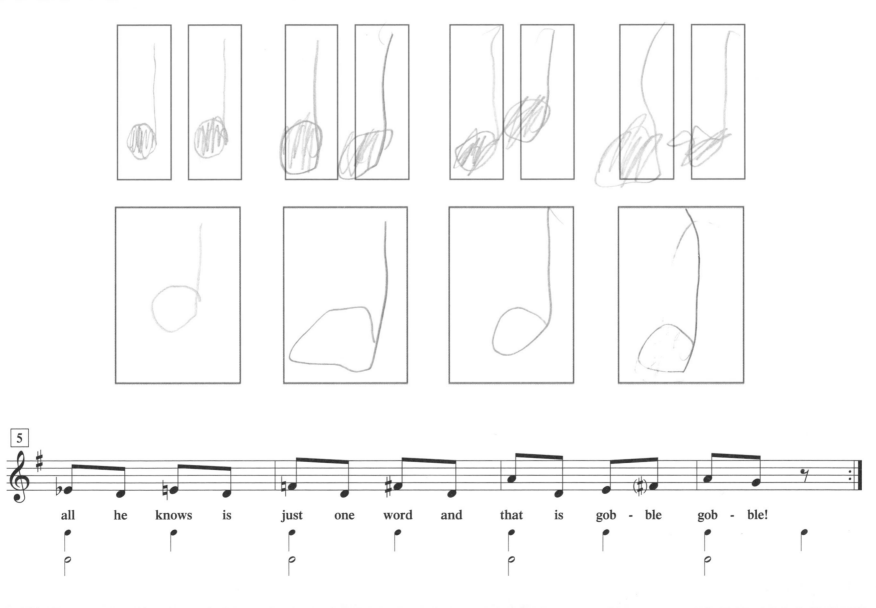

all he knows is just one word and that is gob - ble gob - ble!

Your teacher will use the CD or
sing and play the music (bottom of p. 33).

1. Squeak the mouse rhythms with your voice.

2. Repeat and play the mouse rhythms on a **high E key**.

Mouse Rhythms
Quarter and Half Note Patterns

**1. Monsieur Mouse runs through the house
and this is what I hear.**

SQUEAK: e   e   E__   e   e   E__   E__ E__   e   e   E__

**2. Hurry, scurry, Monsieur Mouse
and this is what I hear.**

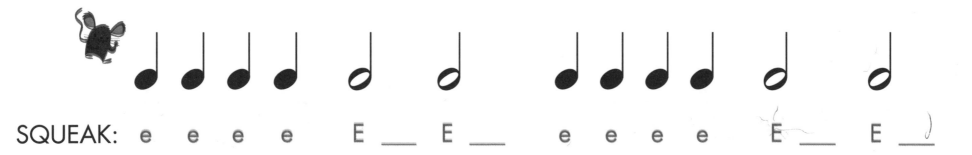

SQUEAK: e   e   e   e   E__ E__   e   e   e   e   E__ E__

3. Down the stairs, behind the chairs, and this is what I hear.

SQUEAK: E___ e e   E___ e e   E___   E___   e e E___

4. Clock is dinging, mouse is singing, this is what I hear.

Write your own squeaky rhythm on the cheese!

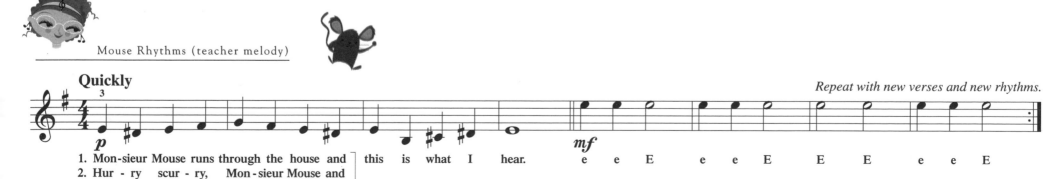

Mouse Rhythms (teacher melody)

Quickly

Repeat with new verses and new rhythms.

p   *mf*

1. Mon-sieur Mouse runs through the house and   this is what I hear.   e e E e e E E E e e E
2. Hur - ry   scur - ry,   Mon - sieur Mouse and
3. Down the stairs, be - hind   the chairs and
4. Clock is   ding - ing, mouse is   sing - ing

LOOK

Sightreading means to play music that you have not seen before.

Eye-training:

1. First, tap the rhythm with your teacher.

2. Decide to play HIGH, MIDDLE, or LOW on the piano. Set a slow, steady beat by saying "*1 - 2 read-y go.*"

3. Once you begin to play, keep going!

Animal Riddles

Can you think of other animals to answer the riddles?

OCTOPUS

KOALA

R.H.
Who   are   you,   what   are   you,   eat - ing   from   the   tree?

Who   are   you,   what   are   you,   swim - ming   in   the   sea?

L.H.

Red Cat, Blue Cat!

Hearing Rhythm Patterns

Ear-training:

1. Your teacher will play **4 steady beats** and then play the rhythm of Red Cat or Blue Cat.

2. Which cat is meowing? Circle that cat!

3. Now YOU play an example from each box for your teacher to guess.

Bass or Treble Sounds

Creating Sounds for Pictures

1. Imagine a sound coming from each picture. Circle the 𝄞 or 𝄢 for the best match.

2. Now create keyboard sounds with your teacher for each picture. Here are some ideas.

f or *p*

high
or
low

short or L - O - N - G

baby birds in a tree

booming thunder

squirrels jumping on the roof

raindrops lightly falling

fire truck honks

tooth fairy flitting around your room

elephants stomping

Melody for a Dragon Kite

Composing a C-D-E Melody

Your friends are visiting the Great Wall of China.

1. Write **C, D,** or **E** inside each box.
2. Play your C-D-E melody with **R.H. fingers 2-3-4**. Hold the last note on each page for two beats. (𝅗𝅥)
3. Now play with **L.H. fingers 4-3-2**.

START

Hold this note.

1-2

FINISH

Hold this note.
1-2

4. Can you play your melody backwards?

Old Mac's Chick
Whole Note

Whole note

o

count: 1-2-3-4

- Draw several **whole notes** below.

- Write 1 2 3 4 or draw four slashes under each.

1. Name the musical term for each numbered part of the chick.

2. Now draw a ♩, ♪, or **o** in each egg.

1. whole note 2. half note 3. quarter note 4. 2-black-keys 5. forte 6. piano

A Game of Beats
Review of ♩♩ and 𝅗𝅥

1. Connect each picture to the note with the SAME number of beats.

2. Find the empty box. Draw your own picture and connect it to the matching note. (Balloons, snowballs, lollipops?)

EX.

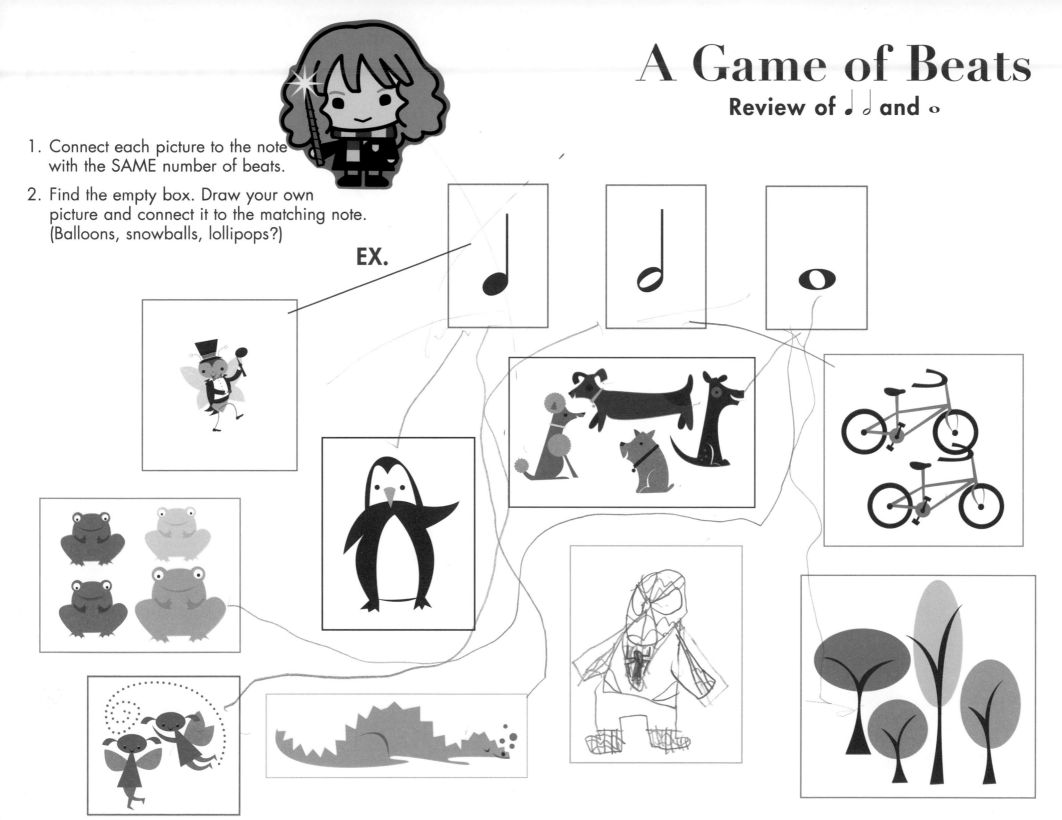

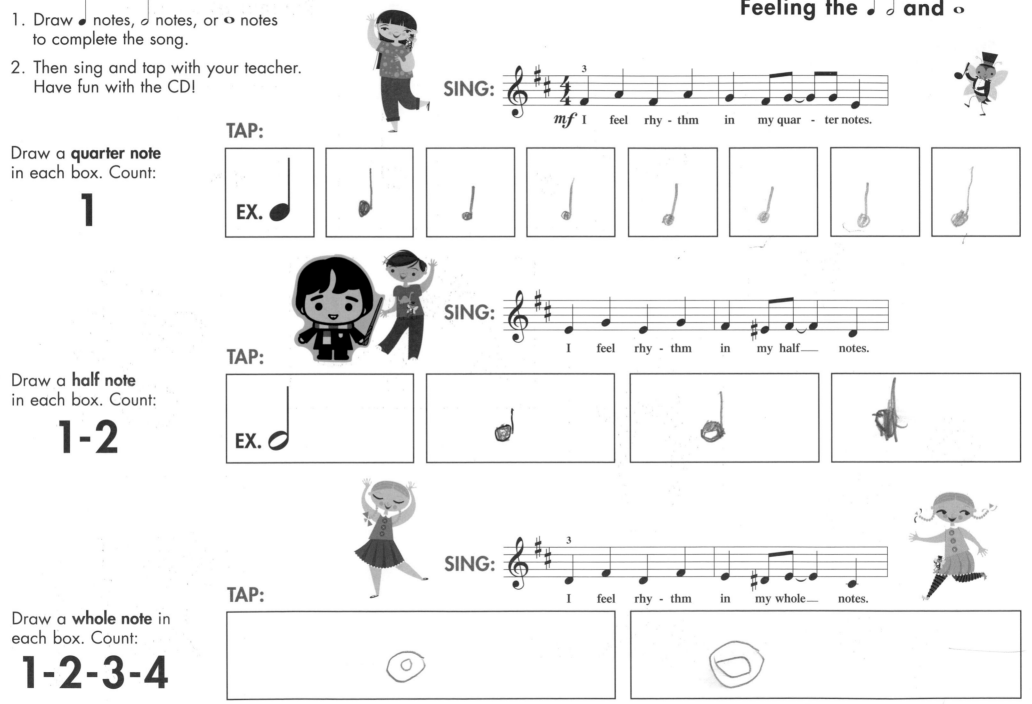

31 I Feel Rhythm

Feeling the ♩♩ ♩ and 𝅝

1. Draw ♩ notes, ♩ notes, or 𝅝 notes to complete the song.

2. Then sing and tap with your teacher. Have fun with the CD!

SING:

mf I feel rhy-thm in my quar-ter notes.

TAP:

Draw a **quarter note** in each box. Count:

1

EX.

SING:

I feel rhy-thm in my half — notes.

TAP:

Draw a **half note** in each box. Count:

1-2

EX.

SING:

I feel rhy-thm in my whole — notes.

TAP:

Draw a **whole note** in each box. Count:

1-2-3-4

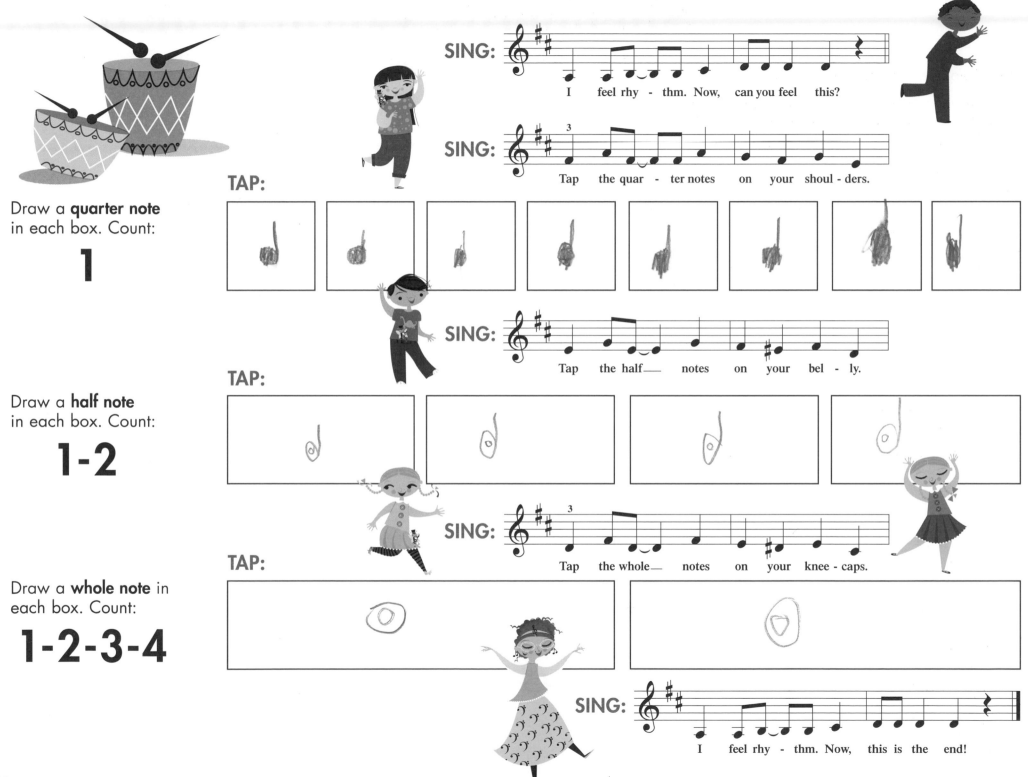

SING: I feel rhy - thm. Now, can you feel this?

SING: Tap the quar - ter notes on your shoul - ders.

Draw a **quarter note** in each box. Count:

1

TAP:

SING: Tap the half — notes on your bel - ly.

Draw a **half note** in each box. Count:

1-2

TAP:

SING: Tap the whole — notes on your knee - caps.

Draw a **whole note** in each box. Count:

1-2-3-4

TAP:

SING: I feel rhy - thm. Now, this is the end!

Shepherds, Count Your Beats

Tapping Rhythms against Each Other

Two shepherds are counting groups of sheep.

1. Can you tap the rhythm of **Shepherd Dallas** while your teacher taps **Shepherd Marta**? Count aloud, "1-2, 1-2, 1, 1, 1, 1,"etc.

2. Then reverse parts.

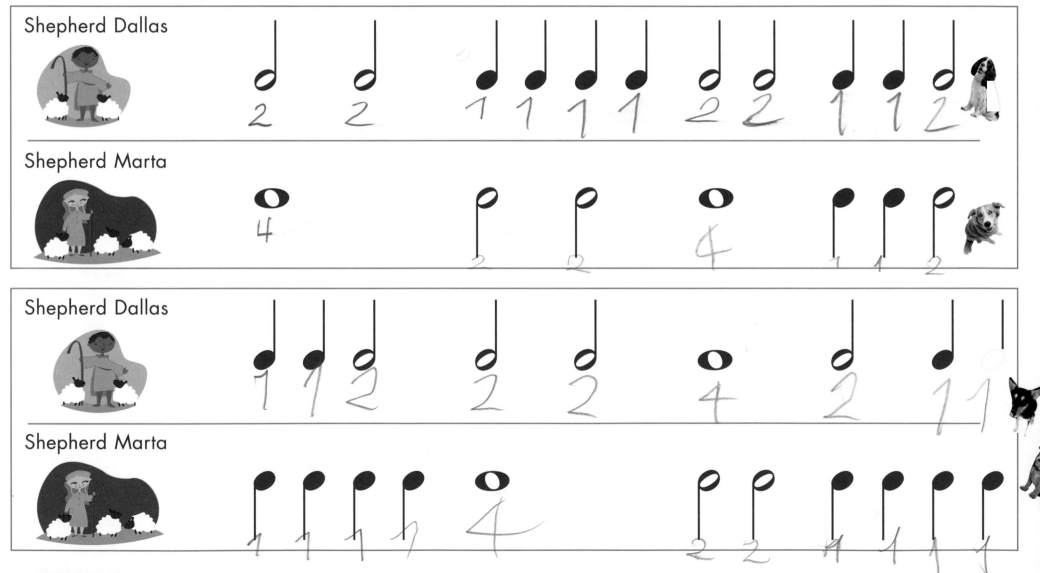

Fruity Faces

Hearing ♪♪ and ◦ Notes

Ear-training:

1. You and your teacher set a SLOW, STEADY beat. Keep tapping the beat as your teacher plays a note.

2. Circle 1, 2, or 4 faces to match the beats you hear.

1.

2.

3.

4.

5.

6.

7.

8.

Teacher: Tap and count 1 - 2 - 3 - 4 before each example. (The examples may be repeated several times and played in any order.)

📖 | LESSON 60-61 (Shepherd, Count Your Sheep)   **45**

Alphabet Castle
Steps in the Alphabet

1. Fill in the castle stairs with the missing letters from the music alphabet.

A B C D E F G

2. Can you find Tap? Draw a silly face in the empty window!

start again with?

start again with?

start again with?

C

A

G

F

B

Royal Mix-up!
Keyboard Steps

1. Circle each keyboard with the alphabet letters in the CORRECT order.

2. Put an X on each keyboard with the letters MIXED-UP! Can you tell your teacher what the letters should be?

Listen to this song and do the motions
with your teacher.

1. Let your **L.H.** hold your heavy **R.H.** forearm.
   Pretend your hand is dangling off a fence post.

2. Use your wrist to gently bounce your R.H.
   up and **down** for the words "bounce, bounce, bounce."

Hangin' on a Fence Post
Flexible Wrist

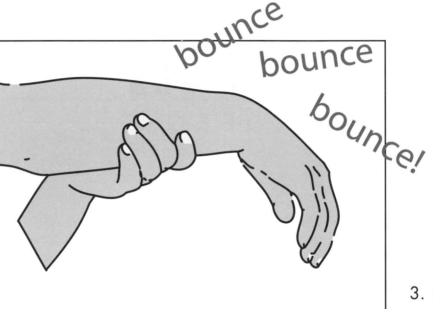

bounce
bounce
bounce!

3. Repeat with your R.H.
   holding your L.H. forearm.

Teacher Melody for Hangin' on a Fence Post:

Lively F

mf I'm talk - in' to my neigh - bor with my right hand hang - in' on a fence post, bounce, bounce, bounce! I'm talk - in' to my neigh - bor with my

F

left hand hang - in' on a fence post, bounce, bounce, bounce! I'm talk - in' to my neigh - bor with both hands hang - in' on a fence post, bounce, bounce, bounce!

Be the Teacher!

Observing Technique

1. Your teacher will demonstrate wrist rainbows from the Lesson Book, page 26 (or pp. 27, 32, or 34).

2. For each WELL DONE rainbow your teacher does, draw a "smiley face" below.

   If your teacher needs improvement, draw a "frowny face." Then, demonstrate to correct your teacher.

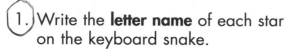

1. Write the **letter name** of each star on the keyboard snake.

2. Now play a duet. Your teacher will help you set a steady beat by first playing **C** and **G back–and–forth**.

3. Keep this steady beat while your teacher sings and plays the melody. End with a **L.H. C**.

Boa Constrictor

Key Review

Student Secondo Part:

R.H.

Repeat over and over.

L.H.

Teacher Melody: For the duet, play the melody HIGH, hands together (one octave apart) on the piano.

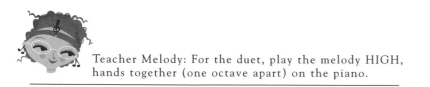

mf I made friends with a bo-a con-stric-tor, bo-a con-stric-tor, bo-a con-stric-tor. | **1.** He's my slip-per-y, slith-er-y friend. Oh, no! | **2.** He tick-led my toe.

FF16

(Student ends on a final C.)

Oh, gee! He tick-led my knee. Oh, fid-dle! He tick-led my mid-dle. Oh, dear! He tick-led my ear. Oh, gig-gle! We wig-gle and we wig-gle!

LESSON 70-71 (Wish I Were a Fish)

Firemen on the C Scale

C Scale Letter Names

1. Say the **letter names** of the first C-scale ladder from bottom to top.

2. Then complete the other C-scale ladders by writing the MISSING letter names.

3. Can you say the letter names for the **C scale backwards** with your *eyes closed*?

C Scale Mystery
C Scale Fingering

1. The twins have a mystery to solve.
   First, write the letter names for the **C scale** on each keyboard.

2. Next, look at the finger number clues.
   Circle **R.H.** or **L.H.** to solve the mystery.

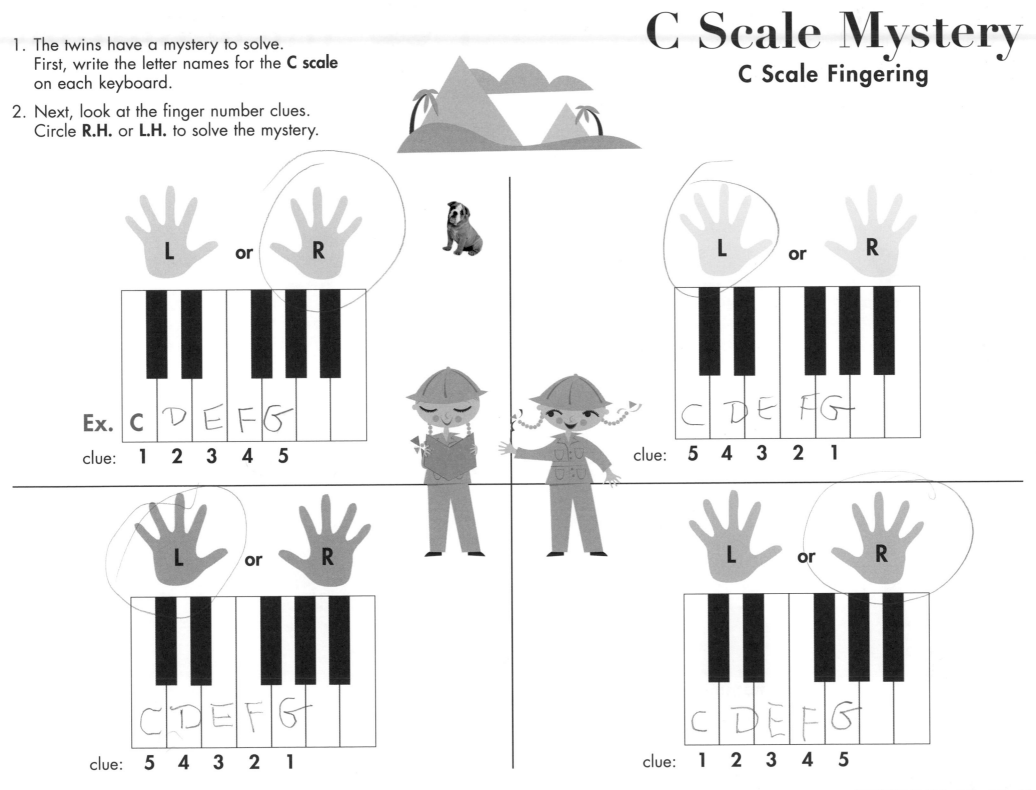

L or **R**

Ex. C D E F G

clue: 1 2 3 4 5

L or **R**

C D E F G

clue: 5 4 3 2 1

L or **R**

C D E F G

clue: 5 4 3 2 1

L or **R**

C D E F G

clue: 1 2 3 4 5

1. Connect each music button to a matching spot in the music.

2. Now tap and count the rhythm! Can you find Tap?

I ♥ Music Buttons
Review of Musical Terms

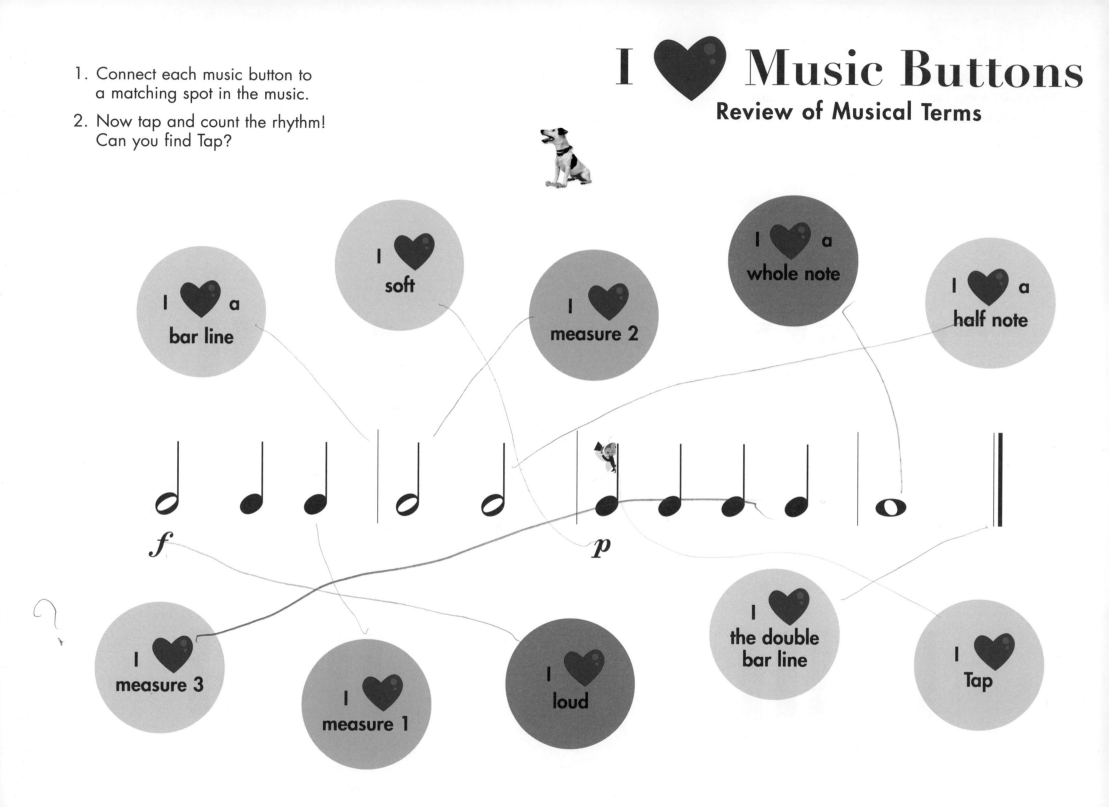

1. Divide this music into measures by drawing a **bar line** after every **4 beats.**

2. Find the C 5-finger scale on the piano. Now sightread the piece.

To begin, set a slow, steady beat:

1 2 3 4, 1 2 ready play!

I Look in the Mirror

Grouping Beats

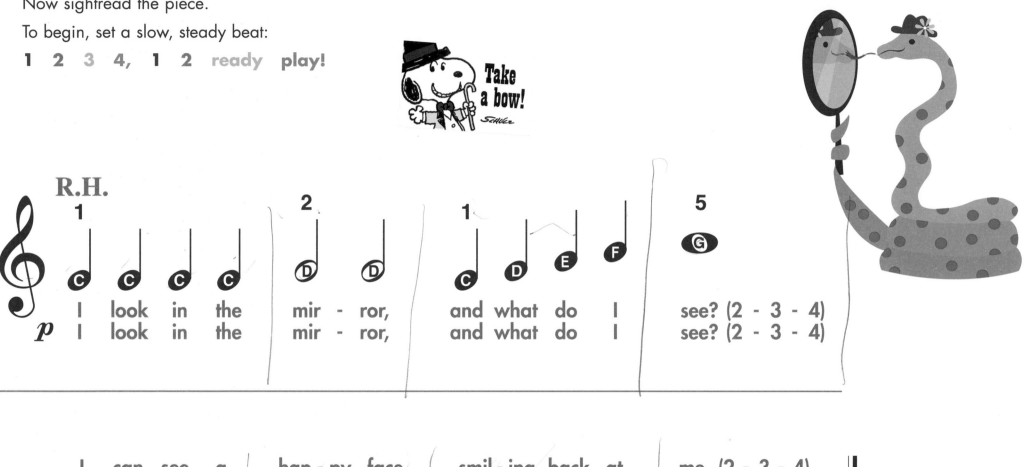

R.H.

p

| I | look | in | the | mir - ror, | and | what | do | I | see? (2 - 3 - 4) |
| I | look | in | the | mir - ror, | and | what | do | I | see? (2 - 3 - 4) |

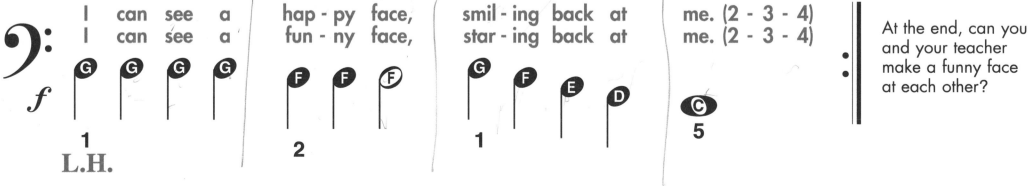

f

| I | can | see | a | hap - py face, | smil - ing | back | at | me. (2 - 3 - 4) |
| I | can | see | a | fun - ny face, | star - ing | back | at | me. (2 - 3 - 4) |

L.H.

At the end, can you and your teacher make a funny face at each other?

Take a bow!

Millie loves splashing in puddles. Do you?

1. Compose your own melody using the **C 5-finger scale.**
2. In each raindrop, write finger number

   1   2   3   4   **or**   5.

3. Then play and say the finger numbers aloud.

I Hear Thunder!
Composing Activity

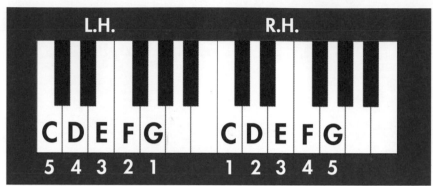

I hear thun - der.   I hear thun - der.   How 'bout you?   How 'bout you?
I see blue skies.   I see blue skies.   Hip, hoo - ray!   Hip, hoo - ray!

L.H.

3 3 3 3   4 4 4 4   5 5 5   2 2 G

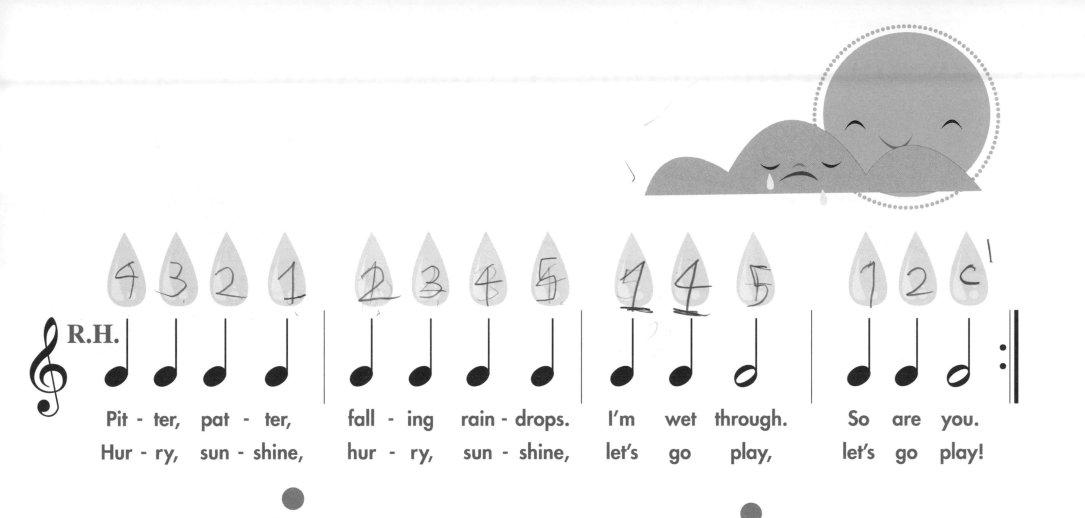

Pit - ter, pat - ter, fall - ing rain - drops. I'm wet through. So are you.

Hur - ry, sun - shine, hur - ry, sun - shine, let's go play, let's go play!

Thunder Beginning:

1. Hold the right-foot pedal down (the damper pedal) and play LOW rumbly sounds with your L.H.

2. Then, lift the pedal and play your song.

Raindrop Ending:

1. Play very HIGH keys quickly with your R.H. Then play slower and slower as the raindrops stop.

2. Take a bow.

A Lesson from Eensie Weensie Spider's Momma
Review of Skills

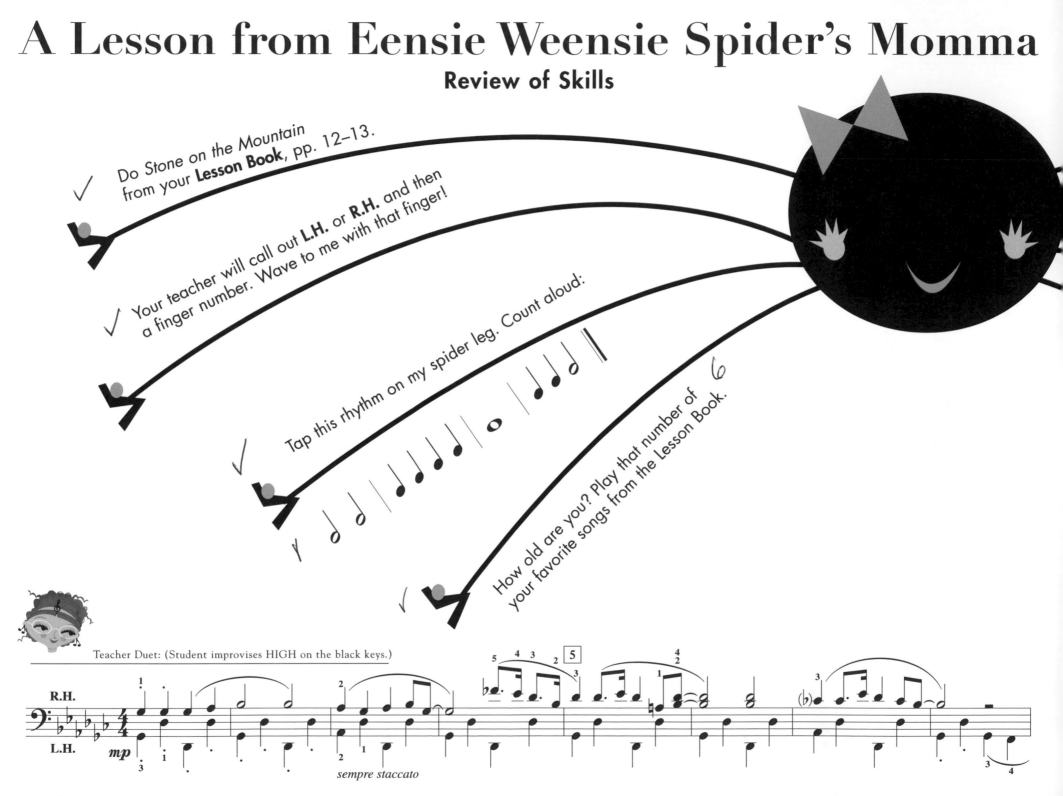

✓ Do *Stone on the Mountain* from your **Lesson Book**, pp. 12–13.

✓ Your teacher will call out **L.H.** or **R.H.** and then a finger number. Wave to me with that finger!

✓ Tap this rhythm on my spider leg. Count aloud:

✓ How old are you? Play that number of your favorite songs from the Lesson Book.

Teacher Duet: (Student improvises HIGH on the black keys.)

R.H.

L.H.   *mp*

sempre staccato

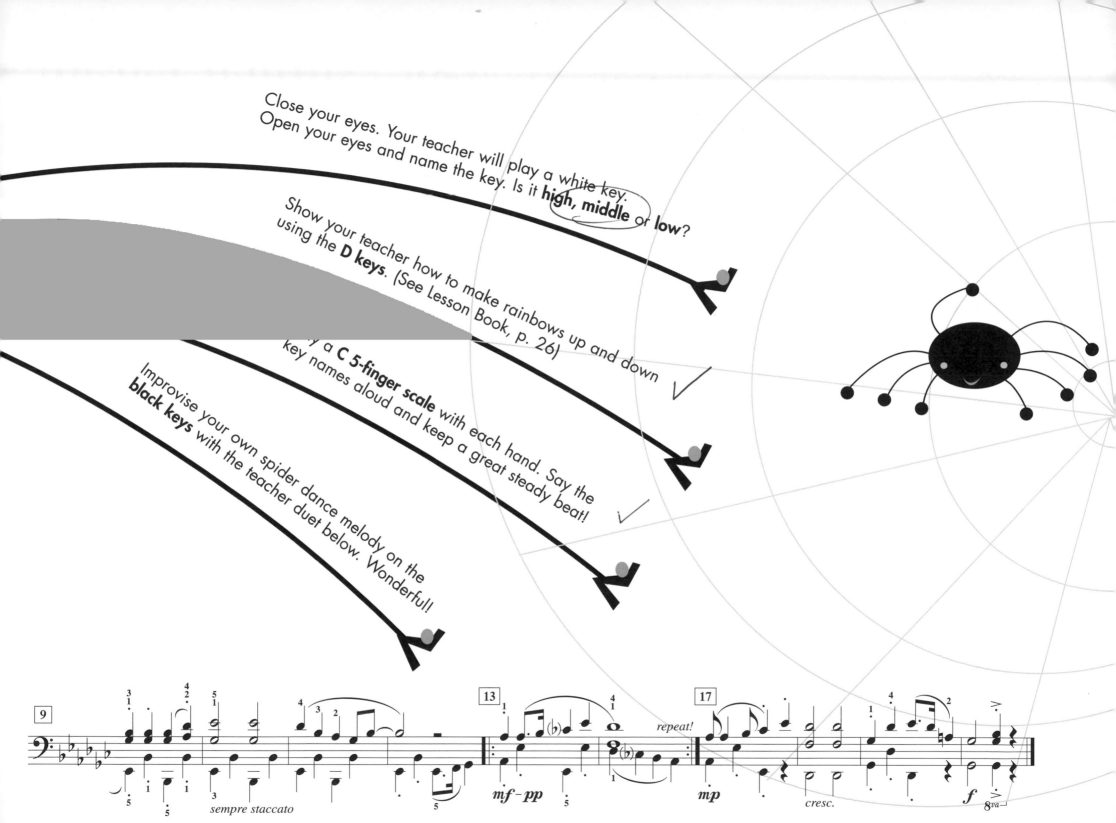

Close your eyes. Your teacher will play a white key.
Open your eyes and name the key. Is it **high, middle** or **low**?

Show your teacher how to make rainbows up and down
using the **D keys**. (See Lesson Book, p. 26)

a **C 5-finger scale** with each hand. Say the
key names aloud and keep a great steady beat!

Improvise your own spider dance melody on the
black keys with the teacher duet below. Wonderful!

C Scale Animal Parade

Pattern Matching and Sightreading

LOOK

Eye-training:

1. Lightly color the measure in each row that is the SAME as the one to the left.

2. Then sightread the measures of music going across to create a **C-scale melody!**

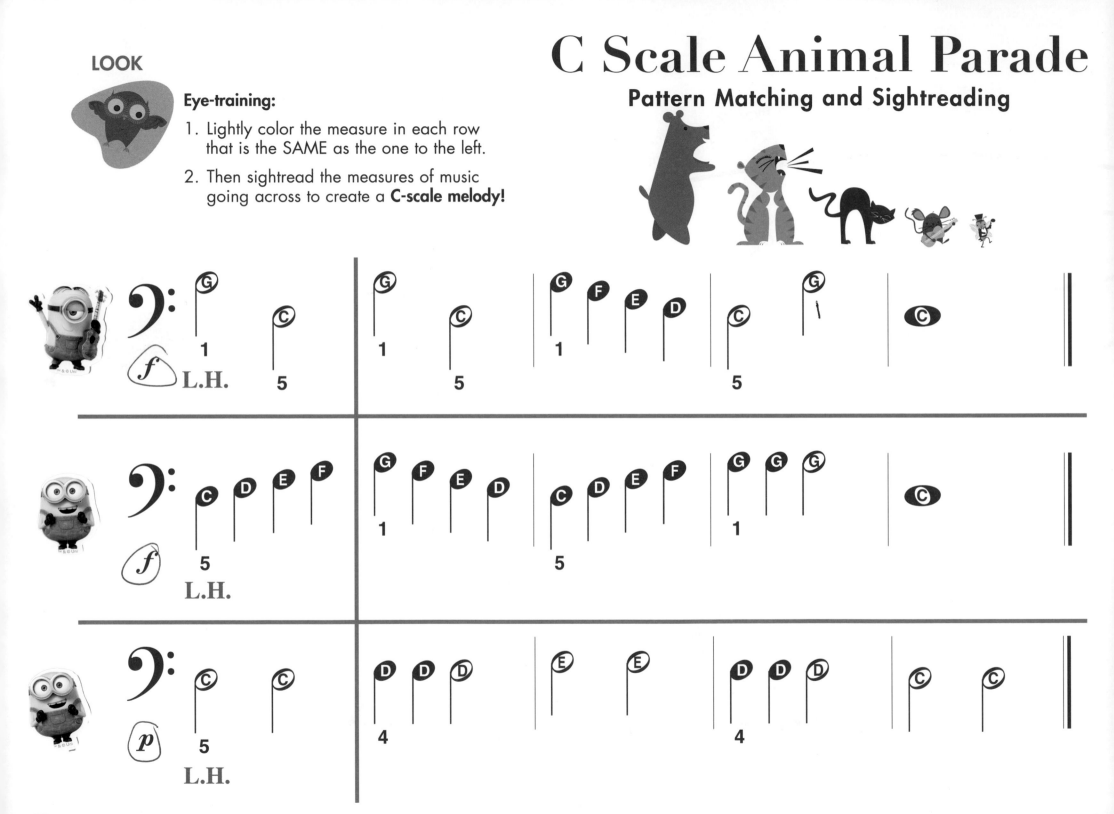

Carlos Says, "Play C-D-E-F-G"

Imitating Melodic Patterns

Ear-training:

1. Place **R.H. fingers 1-2-3-4-5** on a high **C 5-finger scale**.

2. Close your eyes. Your teacher will say, "Carlos says, Play!" and then will play a short pattern using the C 5-finger scale. Play back what you hear!

3. Repeat this activity with **L.H. fingers 5-4-3-2-1**.

R.H. 1 2 3 4 5

C D E F G

L.H. 5 4 3 2 1

Circle a ♩ each time you do this activity!

4. Now make up patterns for your teacher to playback.

For teacher use only (The examples may be played in any order. Continue to play more examples of your own.)

|LESSON 84-85 (Graduation Party) **61**

Alphabet Steps on the Staff
A B C D E F G

1. Circle the arrow to show if the notes are going UP or DOWN.

2. Then draw a line connecting the **empty whole note** to the correct **letter name**.

3. Your teacher may ask you to color the **SPACE** notes **red** and the **LINE** notes **blue**. What color pattern do you see?

Blinker

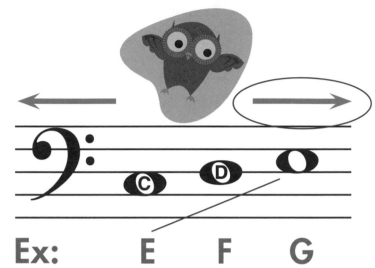

Ex: E   F   G

Carlos

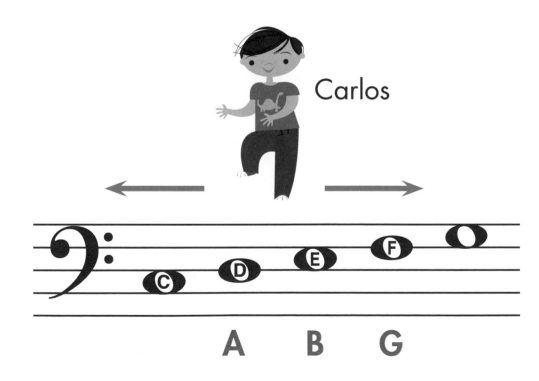

A   B   G

Tap

A   C   E

Congratulations

from Tap, Blinker, and Tucker!

George Turker 9/27/2022

(Sign and join the club!)

You have completed
My First Piano Adventure® Writing Book A.

We can't wait to see you in Writing Book B!

Gotta fly! Come on, Tucker!

FF1